Laws of
Association
Football
Guide for Players
and Referees
1998–1999

Laws of Association Football

Guide for Players and Referees 1998–1999

Authorized by the International
Football Association Board

Revised edition from 1 July 1998

PAN BOOKS

This edition published 1998 by Pan Books
an imprint of Macmillan Publishers Ltd
25 Eccleston Place, London SW1W 9NF
and Basingstoke

Associated companies throughout the world

ISBN 0 330 35245 8

Copyright © Fedération Internationale de Football Association 1998,
Hitzigweg 11, 8030 Zurich, Switzerland
Additional material © The Football Association 1998,
16 Lancaster Gate, London W2 3LW

The right of FIFA and The Football Association to be identified as the
authors of this work has been asserted by them in accordance
with the Copyright, Designs and Patents Act 1988.

9 8 7 6 5 4 3 2 1

A CIP catalogue record for this book is available
from the British Library

Phototypeset by Intype London Ltd
Printed and bound in Great Britain
by Mackays of Chatham PLC

Notes on The Laws of the Game

Modifications

Subject to the agreement of the national association concerned and provided the principles of these Laws are maintained, the Laws may be modified in their application for matches for players of under 16 years of age, for women footballers and for veteran footballers (over 35 years).

Any or all of the following modifications are permissible:

- *size of the field of play*
- *size, weight and material of the ball*
- *width between the goalposts and height of the crossbar from the ground*
- *the duration of the periods of play*
- *number of substitutions*

Further modifications are only allowed with the consent of the International Football Association Board.

Male and Female

References to the male gender in the Laws of the Game in respect of referees, assistant referees, players and officials are for simplification and apply to both males and females.

Key

Throughout the Laws of the Game the following symbols are used:

* Unless covered by the Special Circumstances listed in Law 8 – The Start and Restart of Play

| A single line indicates new Law changes

‖ A double line indicates former International F.A. Board Decisions which are now included in the Laws

WHY WAS **SHEARER** GIVEN SO MUCH ROOM TO **SCORE?**

Flair players need protection if they're to play the kind of football we love to see. That's why referees are a necessary force in football. They enforce the laws of the game. They punish the guilty. But they also protect the innocent. Their presence at every level of the game allows good players to flourish without fear of being clattered every time they collect the ball. Good refereeing encourages good football. And as England prepares for the next World Cup that's exactly what we need. But it's going to take your help. We need referees at every level who will ensure that the next generation of Alan Shearers realise their full potential. For more details phone your local County Football Association, or the FA on 0171 402 7151.

FA REFEREES
WE'RE HERE FOR THE GOOD OF THE GAME

Laws of the Game

Laws of the Game

LAW I – The Field of Play

Dimensions

The field of play must be rectangular. The length of the touch line must be greater than the length of the goal line.

Length: minimum 90 m (100 yds)
              maximum 120 m (130 yds)
Width: minimum 45 m (50 yds)
              maximum 90 m (100 yds)

International Matches

Length: minimum 100 m (110 yds)
              maximum 110 m (120 yds)
Width: minimum 64 m (70 yds)
              maximum 75 m (80 yds)

Field Markings

The field of play is marked with lines. These lines belong to the areas of which they are boundaries.

The two longer boundary lines are called touch lines. The two shorter lines are called goal lines.

All lines are not more than 12 cm (5 ins) wide.

The field of play is divided into two halves by a halfway line.

The centre mark is indicated at the midpoint of the halfway line. A circle with a radius of 9.15 m (10 yds) is marked around it.

The Goal Area

A goal area is defined at each end of the field as follows:

Two lines are drawn at right angles to the goal line, 5.5 m (6 yds) from the inside of each goalpost. These lines extend into the field of play for a distance of 5.5 m (6 yds) and are joined by a line drawn parallel with the goal line. The area bounded by these lines and the goal line is the goal area.

The Penalty Area

A penalty area is defined at each end of the field as follows:

Two lines are drawn at right angles to the goal line, 16.5 m (18 yds) from the inside of each goalpost. These lines extend into the field of play for a distance of 16.5 m (18 yds) and are joined by a line drawn parallel with the goal line. The area bounded by these lines and the goal line is the penalty area.

Within each penalty area a penalty mark is made 11 m (12 yds) from the midpoint between the goalposts and equidistant to them. An arc of a circle with a radius of 9.15 m (10 yds) from each penalty mark is drawn outside the penalty area.

Flagposts

A flagpost, not less than 1.5 m (5 ft) high, with a non-pointed top and a flag is placed at each corner.

Flagposts may also be placed at each end of the halfway line, not less than 1m (1 yd) outside the touch line.

The Corner Arc

A quarter circle with a radius of 1 m (1 yd) from each corner flagpost is drawn inside the field of play.

Goals

Goals must be placed on the centre of each goal line.

They consist of two upright posts equidistant from the corner flagposts and joined at the top by a horizontal crossbar.

The distance between the posts is 7.32 m (8 yds) and the distance from the lower edge of the crossbar to the ground is 2.44 m (8ft).

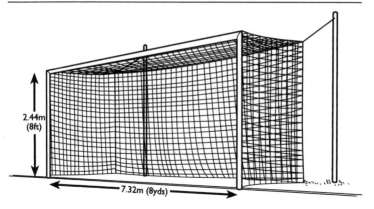

Both goalposts and the crossbar have the same width and depth which do not exceed 12 cm (5 ins). The goal lines are the same width as that of the goalposts and the crossbar. Nets may be attached to the goals and the ground behind the goal, provided that they are properly supported and do not interfere with the goalkeeper.

The goalposts and crossbars must be white.

Safety

Goals must be anchored securely to the ground. Portable goals may only be used if they satisfy this requirement.

The Field of Play

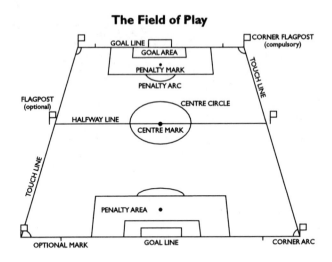

Corner Flagpost

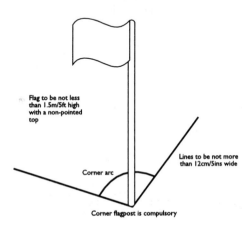

Metric Measurements

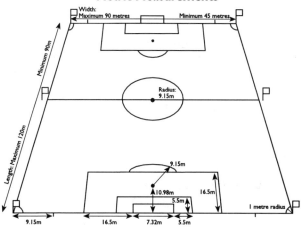

Imperial Measurements

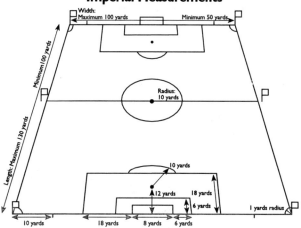

Decisions of the International F.A. Board

Decision I
If the crossbar becomes displaced or broken, play is stopped until it has been repaired or replaced in position. If a repair is not possible, the match is abandoned. The use of a rope to replace the crossbar is not permitted. If the crossbar can be repaired, the match is restarted with a dropped ball at the place where the ball was located when play was stopped. * (see Key)

Decision 2
Goalposts and crossbars must be made of wood, metal or other approved material. Their shape may be square, rectangular, round or elliptical and they must not be dangerous to players.

Decision 3
No kind of commercial advertising, whether real or virtual, is permitted on the field of play and field equipment (including the goal nets and the areas they enclose) from the time the teams enter the field of play until they have left it at half-time and from the time the teams re-enter the field of play until the end of the match. In particular, no advertising material of any kind may be displayed on goals, nets, flagposts or their flags. No extraneous equipment (cameras, microphones, etc.) may be attached to these items.

Decision 4
The reproduction, whether real or virtual, of representative logos or emblems of FIFA, confederations, national associations, leagues, clubs or other bodies, is forbidden on the field of play and field equipment (including the goal nets and the areas they enclose) during playing time, as described in Decision 3.

Decision 5
A mark may be made off the field of play, 9.15 metres (10 yds) from the corner arc and at right angles to the goal lines to ensure that this distance is observed when a corner kick is being taken.

LAW 2 — The Ball

Qualities and Measurements

The ball is:

• *spherical*

• *made of leather or other suitable material*

• *of a circumference of not more than 70 cm (28 ins) and not less than 68 cm (27 ins)*

• *not more than 450 g (16 oz) in weight and not less than 410 g (14 oz) at the start of the match*

• *of a pressure equal to 0.6 – 1.1 atmosphere (600 – 1100 g/cm2) at sea level (8.5 lbs/sq in 15.6 lbs/sq in)*

Replacement of a Defective Ball

If the ball bursts or becomes defective during the course of a match:

• *the match is stopped*

• *the match is restarted by dropping the replacement ball at the place where the first ball became defective * (see Key)*

If the ball bursts or becomes defective whilst not in play at a kick-off, goal kick, corner kick, free kick, penalty kick or throw-in:

• *the match is restarted accordingly*

The ball may not be changed during the match without the authority of the referee.

Decisions of the International F.A. Board

Decision 1

In competition matches, only footballs which meet the minimum technical requirements stipulated in Law 2 are permitted for use.

In FIFA competition matches, and in competition matches organised under the auspices of the confederations, acceptance of a football for use is conditional upon the football bearing one of the following three designations:

the official 'FIFA APPROVED' logo,

or

the official 'FIFA INSPECTED' logo,

or

the reference 'INTERNATIONAL MATCHBALL STANDARD'

Such a designation on a football indicates that it has been tested officially and found to be in compliance with specific technical requirements, different for each category and additional to the minimum specifications stipulated in Law 2. The list of the additional requirements specific to each of the respective categories must be approved by the International F.A. Board. The institutes conducting the tests are subject to the approval of FIFA.

National association competitions may require the use of balls bearing any one of these three designations.

In all other matches the ball used must satisfy the requirements of Law 2.

Decision 2

In FIFA competition matches and in competition matches organised under the auspices of the confederations and national associations, no kind of commercial advertising on the ball is permitted, except for the emblem of the competition, the competition organiser and the authorised trademark of the manufacturer. The competition regulations may restrict the size and number of such markings.

LAW 3 - The Number of Players

Players

A match is played by two teams, each consisting of not more than eleven players, one of whom is the goalkeeper. A match may not start if either team consists of fewer than seven players.

Official Competitions

Up to a maximum of three substitutes may be used in any match played in an official competition organised under the auspices of FIFA, the confederations or the national associations.

The rules of the competition must state how many substitutes may be nominated, from three up to a maximum of seven.

Other Matches

In other matches, up to five substitutes may be used, provided that:

- *the teams concerned reach agreement on a maximum number*
- *the referee is informed before the match*

If the referee is not informed, or if no agreement is reached before the start of the match, no more than three substitutes are allowed.

All Matches

In all matches the names of the substitutes must be given to the referee prior to the start of the match. Substitutes not so named may not take part in the match.

Substitution Procedure

To replace a player by a substitute, the following conditions must be observed:

• *the referee is informed before any proposed substitution is made*

• *a substitute only enters the field of play after the player being replaced has left and after receiving a signal from the referee*

• *a substitute only enters the field of play at the halfway line and during a stoppage in the match*

• *a substitution is completed when a substitute enters the field of play*

• *from that moment, the substitute becomes a player and the player he has replaced ceases to be a player*

• *a player who has been replaced takes no further part in the match*

• *all substitutes are subject to the authority and jurisdiction of the referee, whether called upon to play or not*

Changing the Goalkeeper

Any of the other players may change places with the goalkeeper, provided that:

• *the referee is informed before the change is made*

• *the change is made during a stoppage in the match*

Infringements/Sanctions

If a substitute enters the field of play without the referee's permission:

• *play is stopped*

• *the substitute is cautioned, shown the yellow card and required to leave the field of play*

• *play is restarted with a dropped ball at the place it was located when play was stopped* (see Key)*

If a player changes places with the goalkeeper without the referee's permission before the change is made:

- *play continues*

- *the players concerned are cautioned and shown the yellow card when the ball is next out of play*

For any other infringements of this Law:

- *the players concerned are cautioned and shown the yellow card*

Restart of Play

If play is stopped by the referee to administer a caution:

- *the match is restarted by an indirect free kick, to be taken by a player of the opposing team from the place where the ball was located when play was stopped * (see Key)*

Players and Substitutes Sent Off

A player who has been sent off before the kick-off may be replaced only by one of the named substitutes.

A named substitute who has been sent off, either before the kick-off or after play has started, may not be replaced.

Decisions of the International F.A. Board

Decision 1
Subject to the overriding conditions of Law 3, the minimum number of players in a team is left to the discretion of national associations. The Board is of the opinion, however, that a match should not continue if there are fewer than seven players in either team.

Decision 2
The coach may convey tactical instructions to the players during the match. He and the other officials must remain within the confines of the technical area, where such an area is provided, and they must behave in a responsible manner.

LAW 4 – The Players' Equipment

Safety

A player must not use equipment or wear anything which is dangerous to himself or another player (including any kind of jewellery).

Basic Equipment

The basic compulsory equipment of a player is:

- *a jersey or shirt*
- *shorts - if thermal undershorts are worn, they are of the same main colour as the shorts*
- *stockings*
- *shinguards*
- *footwear*

Shinguards

- *are covered entirely by the stockings*
- *are made of a suitable material (rubber, plastic, or similar substances)*
- *provide a reasonable degree of protection*

Goalkeepers

- *each goalkeeper wears colours which distinguish him from the other players, the referee and the assistant referees*

Infringements/Sanctions

For any infringement of this Law:

- *play need not be stopped*
- *the player at fault is instructed by the referee to leave the field of play to correct his equipment*

• *the player leaves the field of play when the ball next ceases to be in play, unless he has already corrected his equipment*

• *any player required to leave the field of play to correct his equipment does not re-enter without the referee's permission*

• *the referee checks that the player's equipment is correct before allowing him to re-enter the field of play*

• *the player is only allowed to re-enter the field of play when the ball is out of play*

A player who has been required to leave the field of play because of an infringement of this Law and who enters (or re-enters) the field of play without the referee's permission is cautioned and shown the yellow card.

Restart of Play

If play is stopped by the referee to administer a caution:

• *the match is restarted by an indirect free kick taken by a player of the opposing side, from the place where the ball was located when the referee stopped the match * (see Key)*

LAW 5 – The Referee

The Authority of the Referee

Each match is controlled by a referee who has full authority to enforce the Laws of the Game in connection with the match to which he has been appointed.

Powers and Duties

The Referee:

- *enforces the Laws of the Game*

- *controls the match in co-operation with the assistant referees and, where applicable, with the fourth official*

- *ensures that the ball meets the requirements of Law 2*

- *ensures that the players' equipment meets the requirements of Law 4*

- *acts as timekeeper and keeps a record of the match*

- *stops, suspends or terminates the match, at his discretion, for any infringements of the Laws*

- *stops, suspends or terminates the match because of outside interference of any kind*

- *stops the match if, in his opinion, a player is seriously injured and ensures that he is removed from the field of play*

- *allows play to continue until the ball is out of play if a player is, in his opinion, only slightly injured*

- *ensures that any player bleeding from a wound leaves the field of play. The player may only return on receiving a signal from the referee, who must be satisfied that the bleeding has stopped*

- *allows play to continue when the team against which an offence has been committed will benefit from such an advantage and penalises the original offence if the anticipated advantage does not ensue at that time*

• *punishes the more serious offence when a player commits more than one offence at the same time*

• *takes disciplinary action against players guilty of cautionable and sending-off offences. He is not obliged to take this action immediately but must do so when the ball next goes out of play*

• *takes action against team officials who fail to conduct themselves in a responsible manner and may, at his discretion, expel them from the field of play and its immediate surrounds*

• *acts on the advice of assistant referees regarding incidents which he has not seen*

• *ensures that no unauthorised persons enter the field of play*

• *restarts the match after it has been stopped*

• *provides the appropriate authorities with a match report which includes information on any disciplinary action taken against players, and/or team officials and any other incidents which occurred before, during or after the match*

Decisions of the Referee

The decisions of the referee regarding facts connected with play are final.

The referee may only change a decision on realising that it is incorrect or, at his discretion, on the advice of an assistant referee, provided that he has not restarted play.

Decisions of the International F.A. Board

Decision I
A referee (or where applicable, an assistant referee or fourth official) is not held liable for:

any kind of injury suffered by a player, official or spectator

any damage to property of any kind

any other loss suffered by any individual, club, company, association or other body, which is due or which may be due to any decision which he may take under the terms of the Laws of the Game or in respect of the normal procedures required to hold, play and control a match.

This may include:

• *a decision that the condition of the field of play or its surrounds or that the weather conditions are such as to allow or not to allow a match to take place*

• *a decision to abandon a match for whatever reason*

• *a decision as to the condition of the fixtures or equipment used during a match including the goalposts, crossbar, flagposts and the ball*

• *a decision to stop or not to stop a match due to spectator interference or any problem in the spectator area*

• *a decision to stop or not to stop play to allow an injured player to be removed from the field of play for treatment*

• *a decision to request or insist that an injured player be removed from the field of play for treatment*

• *a decision to allow or not to allow a player to wear certain apparel or equipment*

• *a decision (in so far as this may be his responsibility) to allow or not to allow any persons (including team or stadium officials, security officers, photographers or other media representatives) to be present in the vicinity of the field of play*

• *any other decision which he may take in accordance with the Laws of the Game or in conformity with his duties under the terms of FIFA, confederation, national association or league rules or regulations under which the match is played*

Decision 2

In tournaments or competitions where a fourth official is appointed, his role and duties must be in accordance with the guidelines approved by the International F.A. Board.

Decision 3

Facts connected with play shall include whether a goal is scored or not and the result of the match.

Duties

Two assistant referees are appointed whose duties, subject to the decision of the referee, are to indicate:

- *when the whole of the ball has passed out of the field of play*

- *which side is entitled to a corner kick, goal kick or throw-in*

- *when a player may be penalised for being in an offside position*

- *when a substitution is requested*

- *when misconduct or any other incident has occurred out of the view of the referee*

Assistance

The assistant referees also assist the referee to control the match in accordance with the Laws of the Game.

In the event of undue interference or improper conduct, the referee will relieve an assistant referee of his duties and make a report to the appropriate authorities.

LAW 7 – The Duration of the Match

Periods of Play

The match lasts two equal periods of 45 minutes, unless otherwise mutually agreed between the referee and the two participating teams. Any agreement to alter the periods of play (for example to reduce each half to 40 minutes because of insufficient light) must be made before the start of play and must comply with competition rules.

Half-Time Interval

Players are entitled to an interval at half-time.

The half-time interval must not exceed 15 minutes.

Competition rules must state the duration of the half-time interval.

The duration of the half-time interval may be altered only with the consent of the referee.

Allowance for Time Lost

Allowance is made in either period for all time lost through:

- *substitution(s)*
- *assessment of injury to players*
- *removal of injured players from the field of play for treatment*
- *wasting time*
- *any other cause*

The allowance for time lost is at the discretion of the referee.

Penalty Kick

If a penalty kick has to be taken or retaken, the duration of either half is extended until the penalty kick is completed.

Extra Time

Competition rules may provide for two further equal periods to be played. The conditions of Law 8 will apply.

Abandoned Match

An abandoned match is replayed unless the competition rules provide otherwise.

LAW 8 – The Start and Restart of Play

Preliminaries

A coin is tossed and the team which wins the toss decides which goal it will attack in the first half of the match.

The other team takes the kick-off to start the match.

The team which wins the toss takes the kick-off to start the second half of the match.

In the second half of the match the teams change ends and attack the opposite goals.

Kick-off

A kick-off is a way of starting or restarting play:

- *at the start of the match*

- *after a goal has been scored*

- *at the start of the second half of the match*

- *at the start of each period of extra time, where applicable*

A goal may be scored directly from the kick-off.

Procedure

- *all players are in their own half of the field*

- *the opponents of the team taking the kick-off are at least 9.15 m (10 yds) from the ball until it is in play*

- *the ball is stationary on the centre mark*

- *the referee gives a signal*

- *the ball is in play when it is kicked and moves forward*

- *the kicker does not touch the ball a second time until it has touched another player*

After a team scores a goal, the kick-off is taken by the other team.

Infringements/Sanctions

If the kicker touches the ball a second time before it has touched another player:

- *an indirect free kick is awarded to the opposing team to be taken from the place where the infringement occurred* (see Key)*

For any other infringement of the kick-off procedure:

- *the kick-off is retaken*

Dropped Ball

A dropped ball is a way of restarting the match after a temporary stoppage which becomes necessary, while the ball is in play, for any reason not mentioned elsewhere in the Laws of the Game.

Procedure

The referee drops the ball at the place where it was located when play was stopped.* (see Key)

Play restarts when the ball touches the ground.

Infringements/Sanctions

The ball is dropped again:

- *if it is touched by a player before it makes contact with the ground*

- *if the ball leaves the field of play after it makes contact with the ground, without a player touching it*

Special Circumstances

A free kick awarded to the defending team inside its own goal area is taken from any point within the goal area.

An indirect free kick awarded to the attacking team in its opponents' goal area is taken from the goal area line parallel to the goal line at the point nearest to where the infringement occurred.

A dropped ball to restart the match after play has been temporarily stopped inside the goal area takes place on the goal area line parallel to the goal line at the point nearest to where the ball was located when play was stopped.

LAW 9 – The Ball In and Out of Play

Ball Out of Play

The ball is out of play when:

• *it has wholly crossed the goal line or touch line whether on the ground or in the air*

• *play has been stopped by the referee*

Ball In Play

The ball is in play at all other times, including when:

• *it rebounds from a goalpost, crossbar or corner flagpost and remains in the field of play*

• *it rebounds from either the referee or an assistant referee when they are on the field of play*

LAW 10 - The Method of Scoring

Goal Scored

A goal is scored when the whole of the ball passes over the goal line, between the goalposts and under the crossbar, provided that no infringement of the Laws of the Game has been committed previously by the team scoring the goal.

Winning Team

The team scoring the greater number of goals during a match is the winner. If both teams score an equal number of goals, or if no goals are scored, the match is drawn.

Competition Rules

For matches ending in a draw, competition rules may state provisions involving extra time, or other procedures approved by the International F.A. Board to determine the winner of a match.

LAW 11 - Offside

Offside Position

It is not an offence in itself to be in an offside position.

A player is in an offside position if:

• *he is nearer to his opponents' goal line than both the ball and the second last opponent*

A player is not in an offside position if:

• *he is in his own half of the field of play*

or

• *he is level with the second last opponent*

or

• *he is level with the last two opponents*

Offence

A player in an offside position is only penalised if, at the moment the ball touches or is played by one of his team, he is, in the opinion of the referee, involved in active play by:

• *interfering with play*

or

• *interfering with an opponent*

or

• *gaining an advantage by being in that position*

No Offence

There is no offside offence if a player receives the ball directly from:

• *a goal kick*

or

- *a throw-in*

or

- *a corner kick*

Infringements/Sanctions

For any offside offence, the referee awards an indirect free kick to the opposing team to be taken from the place where the infringement occurred.* (see Key)

LAW 12 – Fouls and Misconduct

Fouls and misconduct are penalised as follows:

Direct Free Kick

A direct free kick is awarded to the opposing team if a player commits any of the following six offences in a manner considered by the referee to be careless, reckless or using excessive force:

- *kicks or attempts to kick an opponent*

- *trips or attempts to trip an opponent*

- *jumps at an opponent*

- *charges an opponent*

- *strikes or attempts to strike an opponent*

- *pushes an opponent*

A direct free kick is also awarded to the opposing team if a player commits any of the following four offences:

- *tackles an opponent to gain possession of the ball, making contact with the opponent before touching the ball*

- *holds an opponent*

- *spits at an opponent*

- *handles the ball deliberately (except for the goalkeeper within his own penalty area)*

A direct free kick is taken from where the offence occurred.* (see Key)

Penalty Kick

A penalty kick is awarded if any of the above ten offences is committed by a player inside his own penalty area, irrespective of the position of the ball, provided it is in play.

Indirect Free Kick

An indirect free kick is awarded to the opposing team if a goalkeeper, inside his own penalty area, commits any of the following five offences:

* *takes more than four steps while controlling the ball with his hands, before releasing it from his possession*

* *touches the ball again with his hands after it has been released from his possession and has not touched any other player*

* *touches the ball with his hands after it has been deliberately kicked to him by a team-mate*

* *touches the ball with his hands after he has received it directly from a throw-in taken by a team-mate*

* *wastes time*

An indirect free kick is also awarded to the opposing team if a player, in the opinion of the referee:

* *plays in a dangerous manner*

* *impedes the progress of an opponent*

* *prevents the goalkeeper from releasing the ball from his hands*

* *commits any other offence, not previously mentioned in Law 12, for which play is stopped to caution or dismiss a player*

The indirect free kick is taken from where the offence occurred.*
(see Key)

Disciplinary Sanctions

Cautionable Offences

A player is cautioned and shown the yellow card if he commits any of the following seven offences:

1. is guilty of unsporting behaviour

2. shows dissent by word or action

3. persistently infringes the Laws of the Game

4. delays the restart of play

5. fails to respect the required distance when play is restarted with a corner kick or free kick

6. enters or re-enters the field of play without the referee's permission

7. deliberately leaves the field of play without the referee's permission

Sending-Off Offences

A player is sent off and shown the red card if he commits any of the following seven offences:

1. is guilty of serious foul play

2. is guilty of violent conduct

3. spits at an opponent or any other person

4. denies the opposing team a goal or an obvious goal-scoring opportunity by deliberately handling the ball (this does not apply to a goalkeeper within his own penalty area)

5. denies an obvious goal-scoring opportunity to an opponent moving towards the player's goal by an offence punishable by a free kick or a penalty kick

6. uses offensive, insulting or abusive language

7. receives a second caution in the same match

Decisions of the International F.A. Board

Decision 1

A penalty kick is awarded if, while the ball is in play, the goalkeeper, inside his own penalty area, strikes or attempts to strike an opponent by throwing the ball at him.

Decision 2

A player who commits a cautionable or sending-off offence, either on or off the field of play, whether directed towards an opponent, a team-mate, the referee, an assistant referee or any other person, is disciplined according to the nature of the offence committed.

Decision 3

The goalkeeper is considered to be in control of the ball by touching it with any part of his hand or arms. Possession of the ball includes the goalkeeper deliberately parrying the ball, but does not include the circumstances where, in the opinion of the referee, the ball rebounds accidentally from the goalkeeper, for example after he has made a save.

The goalkeeper is considered to be guilty of time-wasting if he holds the ball in his hands or arms for more than 5–6 seconds.

Decision 4

Subject to the terms of Law 12, a player may pass the ball to his own goalkeeper using his head or chest or knee, etc. If, however, in the opinion of the referee, a player uses a deliberate trick while the ball is in play in order to circumvent the Law, the player is guilty of unsporting behaviour. He is cautioned, shown the yellow card and an indirect free kick is awarded to the opposing team from the place where the infringement occurred. * (see Key)

A player using a deliberate trick to circumvent the Law while he is taking a free kick, is cautioned for unsporting behaviour and shown the yellow card. The free kick is retaken.

In such circumstances, it is irrelevant whether the goalkeeper sub-sequently touches the ball with his hands or not. The offence is commit-ted by the player in attempting to circumvent both the letter and the spirit of Law 12.

Decision 5

A tackle from behind which endangers the safety of an opponent must be sanctioned as serious foul play.

LAW 13 – Free Kicks

Types of Free Kicks

Free kicks are either direct or indirect.

For both direct and indirect free kicks, the ball must be stationary when the kick is taken and the kicker does not touch the ball a second time until it has touched another player.

The Direct Free Kick

• *if a direct free kick is kicked directly into the opponents' goal, a goal is awarded*

• *if a direct free kick is kicked directly into the team's own goal, a corner kick is awarded to the opposing team*

The Indirect Free Kick

Signal

The referee indicates an indirect free kick by raising his arm above his head. He maintains his arm in that position until the kick has been taken and the ball has touched another player or goes out of play.

Ball Enters the Goal

A goal can be scored only if the ball subsequently touches another player before it enters the goal.

• *if an indirect free kick is kicked directly into the opponents' goal, a goal kick is awarded*

• *if an indirect free kick is kicked directly into the team's own goal, a corner kick is awarded to the opposing team*

Position of Free Kick

Free Kick Inside the Penalty Area

Direct or indirect free kick to the defending team:

• *all opponents are at least 9.15 m (10 yds) from the ball*

• *all opponents remain outside the penalty area until the ball is in play*

• *the ball is in play when it is kicked directly beyond the penalty area*

• *a free kick awarded in the goal area is taken from any point inside that area*

Indirect free kick to the attacking team:

• *all opponents are at least 9.15 m (10 yds) from the ball until it is in play, unless they are on their own goal line between the goalposts*

• *the ball is in play when it is kicked and moves*

• *an indirect free kick awarded inside the goal area is taken from that part of the goal area line which runs parallel to the goal line, at the point nearest to where the infringement occurred*

Free Kick Outside the Penalty Area

• *all opponents are at least 9.15 m (10 yds) from the ball until it is in play*

• *the ball is in play when it is kicked and moves*

• *the free kick is taken from the place where the infringement occurred*

Infringements/Sanctions

If, when a free kick is taken, an opponent is closer to the ball than the required distance:

- *the kick is retaken*

If, when a free kick is taken by the defending team from inside its own penalty area, the ball is not kicked directly into play:

- *the kick is retaken*

Free kick taken by a player other than the goalkeeper

If, after the ball is in play, the kicker touches the ball a second time (except with his hands) before it has touched another player:

- *an indirect free kick is awarded to the opposing team, the kick to be taken from the place where the infringement occurred* (see Key)*

If, after the ball is in play, the kicker deliberately handles the ball before it has touched another player:

- *a direct free kick is awarded to the opposing team, the kick to be taken from the place where the infringement occurred* (see Key)*

- *a penalty kick is awarded if the infringement occurred inside the kicker's penalty area*

Free kick taken by the goalkeeper

If, after the ball is in play, the goalkeeper touches the ball a second time (except with his hands), before it has touched another player:

- *an indirect free kick is awarded to the opposing team, the kick to be taken from the place where the infringement occurred* (see Key)*

If, after the ball is in play, the goalkeeper deliberately handles the ball before it has touched another player:

- *a direct free kick is awarded to the opposing team if the infringement occurred outside the goalkeeper's penalty area,* *the kick to be taken from the place where the infringement occurred* (see Key)*

● *an indirect free kick is awarded to the opposing team if the infringement occurred inside the goalkeeper's penalty area, the kick to be taken from the place where the infringement occurred * (see Key)*

Play On – Advantage. Where the referee sees an offence but uses the advantage, he shall indicate that play shall continue

Indirect Free-kick. This signal shall be maintained until the kick has been taken and retained until the ball has been played or touched by another player or goes out of play

Direct Free-kick. The hand and arm clearly indicate the direction

Penalty-kick. The referee clearly indicates the penalty-mark, but there is no need to run towards it

al-kick

rner-kick

Caution or Expulsion. With the ~~system in operation, the card shall~~ shown in the manner illustrated. T~~he~~ player's identity *must* be recorded ~~at~~ the time

Off-side. Flag held upright to ind~~icate~~ Off-side

-side. When the referee stops play, ~~~tant referee indicates position of ~~~side of the field

-side. Position on near side of the ~~~~

Off-side. Position near the centre
the field

Throw-in

k view of the assistant referee
alling to the referee for a
stitution to be made

nt view of the assistant referee
alling to the referee when a
stitute is waiting at the
ch-line

Corner-kick. The assistant referee may first need to signal that the ball has gone of play if there is any doubt. He should also look at the referee in case he has alre made his own decision which may be different from the assistant referee's

Goal-kick

LAW 14 - The Penalty Kick

A penalty kick is awarded against a team which commits one of the ten offences for which a direct free kick is awarded, inside its own penalty area and while the ball is in play.

A goal may be scored directly from a penalty kick.

Additional time is allowed for a penalty kick to be taken at the end of each half or at the end of periods of extra time.

Position of the Ball and the Players

The ball:

• *is placed on the penalty mark*

The player taking the penalty kick:

• *is properly identified*

The defending goalkeeper:

• *remains on his goal line, facing the kicker, between the goal-posts until the ball has been kicked*

The players other than the kicker are located:

• *inside the field of play*

• *outside the penalty area*

• *behind the penalty mark*

• *at least 9.15 m (10 yds) from the penalty mark*

The Referee

• *does not signal for a penalty kick to be taken until the players have taken up position in accordance with the Law*

• *decides when a penalty kick has been completed*

Procedure

- *the player taking the penalty kicks the ball forward*

- *he does not play the ball a second time until it has touched another player*

- *the ball is in play when it is kicked and moves forward*

When a penalty kick is taken during the normal course of play, or time has been extended at half-time or full time to allow a penalty kick to be taken or retaken, a goal is awarded if, before passing between the goalposts and under the crossbar:

- *the ball touches either or both of the goalposts and/or the crossbar, and/or the goalkeeper*

Infringements/Sanctions

If the referee gives the signal for a penalty kick to be taken and, before the ball is in play, one of the following situations occurs:

The player taking the penalty kick infringes the Laws of the Game:

- *the referee allows the kick to proceed*

- *if the ball enters the goal, the kick is retaken*

- *if the ball does not enter the goal, the kick is not retaken*

The goalkeeper infringes the Laws of the Game:

- *the referee allows the kick to proceed*

- *if the ball enters the goal, a goal is awarded*

- *if the ball does not enter the goal, the kick is retaken*

A team-mate of the player taking the kick enters into the penalty area or moves in front of or within 9.15 m (10 yds) of the penalty mark:

- *the referee allows the kick to proceed*

- *if the ball enters the goal, the kick is retaken*

- *if the ball does not enter the goal, the kick is not retaken*

- *if the ball rebounds from the goalkeeper, the crossbar or the goal post and is touched by this player, the referee stops play and restarts the match with an indirect free kick to the defending team.*

A team-mate of the goalkeeper enters the penalty area or moves in front of or within 9.15 m (10 yds) of the penalty mark:

- *the referee allows the kick to proceed*

- *if the ball enters the goal, a goal is awarded*

- *if the ball does not enter the goal, the kick is retaken*

A player of both the defending team and the attacking team infringe the Laws of the Game:

- *the kick is retaken*

If, after the penalty kick has been taken:

The kicker touches the ball a second time (except with his hands) before it has touched another player:

- *an indirect free kick is awarded to the opposing team, the kick to be taken from the place where the infringement occurred* (see Key)*

The kicker deliberately handles the ball before it has touched another player:

- *a direct free kick is awarded to the opposing team, the kick to be taken from the place where the infringement occurred* (see Key)*

The ball is touched by an outside agent as it moves forward:

- *the kick is retaken*

The ball rebounds into the field of play from the goalkeeper, the crossbar or the goalposts, and is then touched by an outside agent:

- *the referee stops play*

• *play is restarted with a dropped ball at the place where it touched the outside agent* (see Key)*

LAW 15 – The Throw-In

A throw-in is a method of restarting play.

A goal cannot be scored directly from a throw-in.

A throw-in is awarded:

• *when the whole of the ball passes over the touch line, either on the ground or in the air*

• *from the point where it crossed the touch line*

• *to the opponents of the player who last touched the ball*

Procedure

At the moment of delivering the ball, the thrower:

• *faces the field of play*

• *has part of each foot either on the touch line or on the ground outside the touch line*

• *uses both hands*

• *delivers the ball from behind and over his head*

The thrower may not touch the ball again until it has touched another player.

The ball is in play immediately it enters the field of play.

Infringements/Sanctions

Throw-in taken by a player other than the goalkeeper

If, after the ball is in play, the thrower touches the ball a second time (except with his hands) before it has touched another player:

• *an indirect free kick is awarded to the opposing team, the kick to be taken from the place where the infringement occurred* (see Key)*

If, after the ball is in play, the thrower deliberately handles the ball before it has touched another player:

• *a direct free kick is awarded to the opposing team, the kick to be taken from the place where the infringement occurred* (see Key)*

• *a penalty kick is awarded if the infringement occurred inside the thrower's penalty area*

Throw-in taken by the goalkeeper

If, after the ball is in play, the goalkeeper touches the ball a second time (except with his hands), before it has touched another player:

• *an indirect free kick is awarded to the opposing team, the kick to be taken from the place where the infringement occurred* (see Key)*

If, after the ball is in play, the goalkeeper deliberately handles the ball before it has touched another player:

• *a direct free kick is awarded to the opposing team if the infringement occurred outside the goalkeeper's penalty area, the kick to be taken from the place where the infringement occurred* (see Key)*

• *an indirect free kick is awarded to the opposing team if the infringement occurred inside the goalkeeper's penalty area, the kick to be taken from the place where the infringement occurred* (see Key)*

If an opponent unfairly distracts or impedes the thrower:

• *he is cautioned for unsporting behaviour and shown the yellow card*

For any other infringement of this Law:

• *the throw-in is taken by a player of the opposing team*

LAW 16 - The Goal Kick

A goal kick is a method of restarting play.

A goal may be scored directly from a goal kick, but only against the opposing team.

A goal kick is awarded when:

• *the whole of the ball, having last touched a player of the attacking team, passes over the goal line, either on the ground or in the air, and a goal is not scored in accordance with Law 10*

Procedure

• *the ball is kicked from any point within the goal area by a player of the defending team*

• *opponents remain outside the penalty area until the ball is in play*

• *the kicker does not play the ball a second time until it has touched another player*

• *the ball is in play when it is kicked directly beyond the penalty area*

Infringements/Sanctions

If the ball is not kicked directly into play beyond the penalty area:

• *the kick is retaken*

Goal kick taken by a player other than the goalkeeper

If, after the ball is in play, the kicker touches the ball a second time (except with his hands) before it has touched another player:

• *an indirect free kick is awarded to the opposing team, the kick to be taken from the place where the infringement occurred* (see Key)*

If, after the ball is in play, the kicker deliberately handles the ball before it has touched another player:

• *a direct free kick is awarded to the opposing team, the kick to be taken from the place where the infringement occurred* (see Key)*

• *a penalty kick is awarded if the infringement occurred inside the kicker's penalty area*

Goal kick taken by the goalkeeper

If, after the ball is in play, the goalkeeper touches the ball a second time (except with his hands) before it has touched another player:

• *an indirect free kick is awarded to the opposing team, the kick to be taken from the place where the infringement occurred* (see Key)*

If, after the ball is in play, the goalkeeper deliberately handles the ball before it has touched another player:

• *a direct free kick is awarded to the opposing team if the infringement occurred outside the goalkeeper's penalty area, the kick to be taken from the place where the infringement occurred* (see Key)*

• *an indirect free kick is awarded to the opposing team if the infringement occurred inside the goalkeeper's penalty area, the kick to be taken from the place where the infringement occurred* (see Key)*

For any other infringement of this Law:

• *the kick is retaken*

LAW 17 - The Corner Kick

A corner kick is a method of restarting play.

A goal may be scored directly from a corner kick, but only against the opposing team.

A corner kick is awarded when:

• *the whole of the ball, having last touched a player of the defending team, passes over the goal line, either on the ground or in the air, and a goal is not scored in accordance with Law 10*

Procedure

• *the ball is placed inside the corner arc at the nearest corner flagpost*

• *the corner flagpost is not moved*

• *opponents remain at least 9.15 m (10 yds) from the ball until it is in play*

• *the ball is kicked by a player of the attacking team*

• *the ball is in play when it is kicked and moves*

• *the kicker does not play the ball a second time until it has touched another player*

Infringements/Sanctions

A corner kick taken by a player other than the goalkeeper

If, after the ball is in play, the kicker touches the ball a second time (except with his hands), before it has touched another player:

• *an indirect free kick is awarded to the opposing team, the kick to be taken from the place where the infringement occurred* (see Key)*

If, after the ball is in play, the kicker deliberately handles the ball before it has touched another player:

• *a direct free kick is awarded to the opposing team, the kick to be taken from the place where the infringement occurred * (see Key)*

• *a penalty kick is awarded if the infringement occurred inside the kicker's penalty area*

Corner kick taken by the goalkeeper

If, after the ball is in play, the goalkeeper touches the ball a second time (except with his hands) before it has touched another player:

• *an indirect free kick is awarded to the opposing team, the kick to be taken from the place where the infringement occurred* (see Key)*

If, after the ball is in play, the goalkeeper deliberately handles the ball before it has touched another player:

• *a direct free kick is awarded to the opposing team if the infringement occurred outside the goalkeeper's penalty area, the kick to be taken from the place where the infringement occurred * (see Key)*

• *an indirect free kick is awarded to the opposing team if the infringement occurred inside the goalkeeper's penalty area, the kick to be taken from the place where the infringement occurred * (see Key)*

For any other infringement:

• *the kick is retaken*

Kicks from the Penalty Mark

Taking kicks from the penalty mark is a method of determining the winning team where competition rules require there to be a winning team after a match has been drawn.

Procedure

• *The referee chooses the goal at which the kicks will be taken.*

• *The referee tosses a coin and the team whose captain wins the toss takes the first kick.*

• *The referee keeps a record of the kicks being taken.*

• *Subject to the conditions explained below, both teams take five kicks.*

• *The kicks shall be taken alternately by the teams.*

• *If, before both teams have taken five kicks, one has scored more goals than the other could score even if it were to complete its five kicks, no more kicks are taken.*

• *If, after both teams have taken five kicks, both have scored the same number of goals, or have not scored any goals, kicks continue to be taken in the same order until one team has scored a goal more than the other from the same number of kicks.*

• *A goalkeeper who is injured while kicks are being taken from the penalty mark and is unable to continue as a goalkeeper may be replaced by a named substitute provided his team has not used the maximum number of substitutes permitted under the competition rules.*

• *With the exception of the foregoing case, only players who are on the field of play at the end of the match, which includes extra time where appropriate, are allowed to take kicks from the penalty mark.*

• *Each kick is taken by a different player, and all eligible players must take a kick before any player can take a second kick.*

• *An eligible player may change places with the goalkeeper at any time when kicks from the penalty mark are being taken.*

• *All players, except the player taking a kick and the two goalkeepers, must remain within the centre circle.*

• *The goalkeeper who is the team mate of the kicker must remain on the field of play, outside the penalty area in which the kicks are being taken, on the goal line where it meets the penalty area boundary line.*

• *Unless otherwise stated, the Laws of the Game, and the International F.A. Board Decisions apply when kicks from the penalty mark are being taken.*

Check-list for Referees

1 Decide at which end the kicks will be taken. This can be an important decision if the supporters of one team are behind one goal and those of the other team are at the opposite goal.

2 The team which wins the toss must take the first kick.

3 Before the kicks begin, ensure that all club officials, etc., have left the field and that only the players are left.

4 Make sure all players, apart from the kicker and the two goalkeepers, are inside the centre circle.

5 Make sure the goalkeeper of the kicker's team stands outside the penalty area.

6 The Laws of the Game, particularly **Law 14** 'The Penalty Kick', apply except where modified by the instructions for the taking of kicks from the penalty mark. Be particularly vigilant therefore for instances of gamesmanship or for infringements by the goalkeeper, e.g. moving before the ball is kicked.

7 Keep a careful record of the kicks taken.

8 Where you have the assistance of Assistant Referees some of those duties may be taken by them, e.g. an Assistant Referee at the centre circle would organize players coming to take the kick while the other Assistant Referee would assist by indicating whether or not the ball has crossed the goal-line.

9 It is very important that the referee organizes the taking of kicks from the penalty mark correctly. Make sure you fully understand the instructions.

10 The taking of kicks from the penalty mark never forms part of an actual match. It is only a method of deciding a winner.

11 If, at the taking of kicks from the penalty mark, the light fails badly and the kicks therefore cannot be completed, the result shall be decided by the tossing of a coin or the drawing of lots.

12 An injured player may be excused from the taking of kicks from the penalty mark.

13 It is the responsibility of each team to select the players who will take the kicks from the penalty mark. The Referee's only duty is to ensure that they are taken correctly.

14 When all the players in a team have taken a kick from the penalty mark, it is not necessary that they follow the same order in taking their second kick as they had for the first series of kicks.

15 If a player who has already been cautioned commits a second cautionable offence at the taking of kicks from the penalty mark, he shall be sent off.

16 If the lights fail at a stadium after extra time but before the taking of kicks from the penalty mark, and if they cannot be repaired in a reasonable time, the referee shall decide the match by tossing a coin or drawing lots.

17 A substitute who has not taken part in the match, including extra time where it is played, may not take part in kicks from the penalty mark, except to replace an injured goalkeeper.

18 After each team has taken 10 kicks from the penalty mark, a team which has had a player sent off may use a player who has already taken a kick for the 11th kick.

19 If at the end of the match some players leave the field of play and fail to return for the taking of kicks from the penalty mark, and are not injured, the Referee will not allow the kicks to be taken and will report the matter to the responsible authorities.

20 If, at the taking of kicks from the penalty mark, or when extended time is being allowed for a penalty-kick to be taken in normal playing time, the ball strikes the goal-post or crossbar, strikes the goalkeeper and enters the goal, a goal shall be awarded.

The Technical Area

The technical area described in Law 3, International F.A. Board Decision no. 2, relates particularly to matches played in stadia with a designated seated area for technical staff and substitutes.

Technical areas may vary between stadia, for example in size or location, and the following notes are issued for general guidance.

• *The technical area extends 1 m (1 yd) on either side of the designated seated area and extends forward up to a distance of 1 m (1 yd) from the touch line.*

• *It is recommended that markings are used to define this area.*

• *The number of persons permitted to occupy the technical area is defined by the competition rules.*

• *The occupants of the technical area are identified before the beginning of the match in accordance with the competition rules.*

• *Only one person at a time is authorised to convey tactical instructions and he must return to his position immediately after giving these instructions.*

• *The coach and other officials must remain within the confines of the technical area except in special circumstances, for example, a physiotherapist or doctor entering the field of play, with the referee's permission, to assess an injured player.*

* *The coach and other occupants of the technical area must behave in a responsible manner.*

- *The fourth official may be appointed under the competition rules and officiates if any of the three match officials is unable to continue.*

- *Prior to the start of the competition, the organiser states clearly whether, if the referee is unable to continue, the fourth official takes over as the match referee or whether the senior assistant referee takes over as referee with the fourth official becoming an assistant referee.*

- *The fourth official assists with any administrative duties before, during and after the match, as required by the referee.*

- *He is responsible for assisting with substitution procedures during the match.*

• *He supervises the replacement footballs, where required. If the match ball has to be replaced during a match, he provides another ball, on the instruction of the referee, thus keeping the delay to a minimum.*

• *He has the authority to check the equipment of substitutes before they enter the field of play. If their equipment does not comply with the Laws of the Game, he informs the assistant referee, who then informs the referee.*

• *The fourth official assists the referee at all times.*

• *After the match, the fourth official must submit a report to the appropriate authorities on any misconduct or other incident which has occurred out of the view of the referee and the assistant referees. The fourth official must advise the referee and his assistants of any report being made.*

Signals by the Referee and Assistant Referees

The signals used in this Memorandum have been approved by the International F.A. Board for use by registered Referees of affiliated National Associations. The signals are simple, universally in use and well understood.

1 While it is not the duty of the Referee to explain or mime any offence that has caused him to give a particular decision, there are times when a **simple gesture** or word of guidance can aid communication and assist toward greater understanding, and gaining more respect, to the mutual benefit of both Referee and players. Improving communication should be encouraged, but the **exaggerated miming** of offences can be undignified and confusing and **should not be used**.

2 An indication by the Referee of the point where a throw-in should be taken may well help a player from taking a throw-in improperly. A call of '**Play On: Advantage**' *confirms to the player that the Referee has not missed a foul*, but has chosen to apply advantage. Even an indication that the ball was minutely deflected by touching another player on its path across a touch line might be helpful in generating a greater understanding between Referee and players. A better understanding will lead to more harmonious relationships.

3 **All signals given by the Referee should be simple, clear and instinctive.** They should be designed to control the game efficiently and to ensure continuous play as far as is possible; they are intended essentially to indicate what the next action in the game should be, not principally to justify that action.

4 An arm pointing to indicate a corner kick, goal kick or foul, and the direction in which the kick is to be taken, will normally be sufficient. **The raised arm to indicate that a free kick is indirect** is clearly understood, but if a player queries politely whether the award is a direct free kick or an indirect free kick, a helpful word from the Referee, in addition to the regular signal, will lead to a better understanding in future.

5 The duties of the Referee and Assistant Referees are set out briefly but clearly in the Laws of the Game, **Laws 5** and **6**.

6 There is a further exposition of co-operation between the Referee and Assistant Referees in the Memorandum explaining the universally adopted system of 'Diagonal Control'.

7 The proper use of the whistle, voice and hand signals by the Referee and the flags by the Assistant Referees should all assist understanding through clear communication.

Co-operation between Assistant Referees and Referee

8 When play has been stopped the Assistant Referee should assist the Referee by signalling in the following manner for the following incidents:

1 Off Side. The Assistant Referee should lower his flag a full arm's length to the positions illustrated, and point across the field of play to indicate the spot from which the kick should be taken. The only exception would be where the Referee has decided to position himself to judge offside when play develops from a corner kick, penalty kick or free kick close to goal.

2 Throw-In. When the ball goes out of play over the touch line on his side of the field, the Assistant Referee should indicate the direction of the throw. He should also signal if the thrower's feet, at the moment of release of the ball, are incorrectly placed.

3 Corner and Goal Kicks. When the whole of the ball goes out of play over the goal line the Assistant Referee should indicate whether a corner kick or a goal kick should be given.

4   Goal. When the Referee indicates that a goal is scored the Assistant Referee should return quickly to his position towards the half way line.

Law 12. If the Assistant Referee senses that the Referee has not seen an infringement he should raise his flag high. If the Referee stops play the Assistant Referee should indicate the direction of the free-kick (direct or indirect), otherwise he shall lower his flag.

5   Substitution. When a substitution is to be made the Assistant Referee nearest the point of substitution shall attract the attention of the Referee by raising his flag as shown in the illustration included in the colour section.

Co-operation between Referee and Assistant Referees – Law 6

In the Laws of the Game set out in the foregoing pages there are no instructions as to the relative positioning of Referee and Assistant Referees during a game. There are, however, instructions in **Laws 5** and **6** with regard to powers and duties of Referees and Assistant Referees which rightly interpreted would mean co-operation. **Law 6** stipulates that two Assistant Referees are appointed, whose duties (subject to the decision of the Referee) are to indicate:–

• when the whole of the ball has passed out of the field of play.

• which side is entitled to a corner kick, goal kick or throw-in.

• when a player may be penalised for being in an offside position.

• when a substitution is requested.

• when misconduct or any other incident has occurred out of the view of the referee.

The assistant referees shall assist the referee to control the match in accordance with the Laws of the Game.

Neutral Assistant Referees

The assistance referred to above is given by ASSISTANT REFEREES. A limitation is placed upon CLUB ASSISTANT REFEREES. They would normally be expected to only indicate when the ball has passed out of the field of play and that a substitution is required. It is appreciated that there must be a different attitude adopted by the Referee in the case of Assistant Referees, because in effect there are THREE officials supervising the play; the REFEREE remains as principal official, but the Assistant Referees are there to assist him to control the game in accordance with the Laws of the Game.

Club Assistant Referees

To get the most effective co-operation from CLUB ASSISTANT REFEREES the following procedure should be adopted:

(1) BOTH Club Assistant Referees should report to the Referee BEFORE the start of the match, and receive his instructions, and be informed that no matter what may be their personal opinion the decision of the Referee is final, and must not be questioned.

(2) The work allotted to them as Club Assistant Referees is to signal WHEN the ball is ENTIRELY over the touch line, subject always to the decisions of the Referee and to inform the referee that a substitution is required.

Keeping in mind their distinctive duties outlined above Referees should decide beforehand exactly WHAT they want their Club Assistant Referees to do, and should be able to tell them distinctly how they can best help him. It is essential that there should be some conference between the three officials BEFORE any match. As the chief of this trio, the Referee must be able to indicate clearly to his assistants how they may best help him. His instructions must be specific, in order to avoid confusion. On their side, the ASSISTANT REFEREES must fully appreciate the Referee's prior authority, and accept his rulings without question, should there be any difference of opinion amongst them. Their relationship to him MUST be one of assistance and neither undue intervention nor opposition.

The Referee will operate the diagonal system of control when his Assistant Referees are neutral. When they are Club Assistant Referees he shall inform them which method he intends to operate. He will co-operate with his Assistant Referees on the following matters and indicate to them:–

(*a*) The time by his watch.

(*b*) The side of the field which each Assistant Referee will take in each half of the match.

(*c*) Their duties prior to the commencement of the game, such as the examination of the appurtenances of the game.

(*d*) Which shall be the senior Assistant Referee in case of need.

(*e*) The position to be taken for corner kicks.

(*f*) The sign that he has noticed his Assistant Referee, but has overruled the indication therefrom.

(*g*) Which action in the throw-in shall be in the province of the Assistant Referee, and which that of the Referee, e.g., many Referees ask their Assistant Referees to watch for foot faults whilst they look for the hand faults.

Referees should not necessarily keep to one diagonal of the field of play. If the state of the ground, wind, sun or other conditions demand a change to the opposite diagonal, a Referee should indicate to his Assistant Referees his intention to make such a change-over, and the Assistant Referees will at once take over the other half of their particular lines. One advantage of such a change of diagonal is that the surface of the ground, next to the touch line, will be less severely worn because the whole length of the field will be utilized.

Other co-operative matters may be added, but it is important that each of these should be known to the three officials.

The following diagrams illustrate the diagonal system of control, and if studied and practised will lead to uniform methods of control.

The Diagonal System of Control

Diagram One

The imaginary diagonal used by the Referee is the line **A–B**; the cross diagonal used by the Assistant Referee is adjusted to the position of the Referee.

If the Referee is near **A**, Assistant Referee **AR2** will be at a point between **M** and **K**; when the Referee is at **B**, Assistant Referee **AR1** will be between **E** and **F**. This gives TWO Officials control of the respective '*danger zones*', one at each side of the field.

Assistant Referee AR1 adopts the REDS as his side; **Assistant Referee AR2** adopts the BLUES. As RED forwards move towards the BLUE goal, Assistant Referee **AR1** keeps up with their foremost man, so in actual practice he will rarely get into RED's half of the field. Similarly Assistant Referee **AR2** keeps up with the foremost BLUE's player, and will rarely get into BLUE's half.

At **corner kicks** or **penalty kicks** the Assistant Referee in that half where the corner kick or penalty kick occurs positions himself at **N** and the Referee takes positions illustrated in **Diagram 4**: Corner kick and **Diagram 9**: Penalty kick.

The Diagonal System **fails** if Assistant Referee **AR2** gets between **G** and **H** when the Referee is at **B**; or when Assistant Referee **AR1** is near **C** or **D** when the referee is at **A**. Then there are TWO Officials at the same place – **this should be avoided.**

(N.B. – Some Referees prefer to use the opposite diagonal, from F to M, in which case the Assistant Referees should adjust their positions accordingly.)

DIAGRAM I

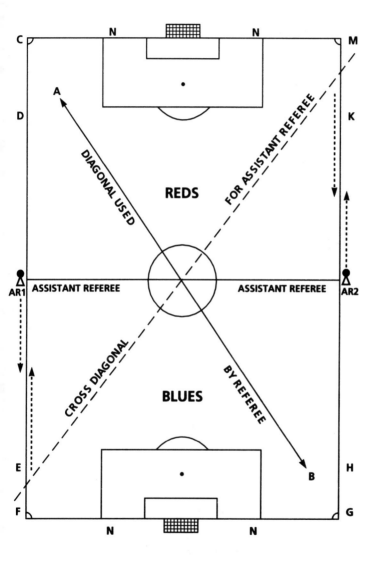

DIAGRAM 2

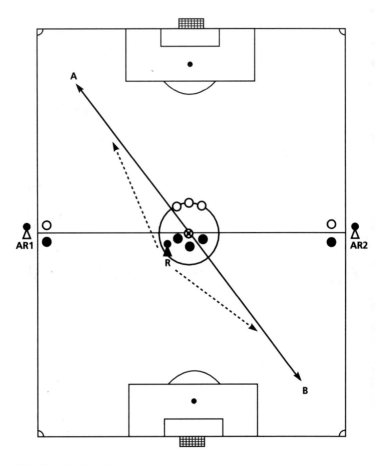

START OF GAME

Position of Referee at Kick-off – R.
Position of Assistant Referees – AR1 and AR2.
Players – ○ and ●.
Diagonal followed by Referee – A —— B.
Referee moves to diagonal along line ←———→ according to direction of attack.
Ball – ⊗.

DIAGRAM 3

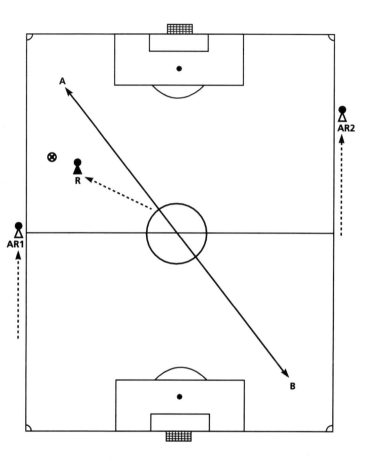

DEVELOPMENT OF ATTACK

(From Diagram 2)

Ball moves out to left wing, Referee (R) slightly off diagonal to be near play.
Assistant Referee (AR2) level with spearhead of attack.
Two officials, therefore, up with play.
Assistant Referee (AR1) in position for clearance and possible counter attack.

DIAGRAM 4

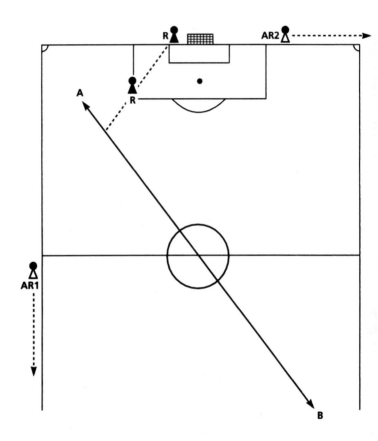

CORNER KICK

Position of officials the same no matter at which corner area the kick is taken.
Referee (R) alongside goal post, or at position shown.

Concerning the position of the Assistant Referee No. 2, in accordance
with the instructions from the Referee the Assistant Referee No. 2 (AR2)
shall be near the corner flag or on the goal line near the corner flag, to
observe whether the ball is properly played, whether the opposing
players are at proper distance (9.15 m), whether the ball is behind the
goal line, or whether incidents have happened possibly hidden from
the Referee.

Assistant Referee (AR1) in position for clearance and possible counter attack.

DIAGRAM 5

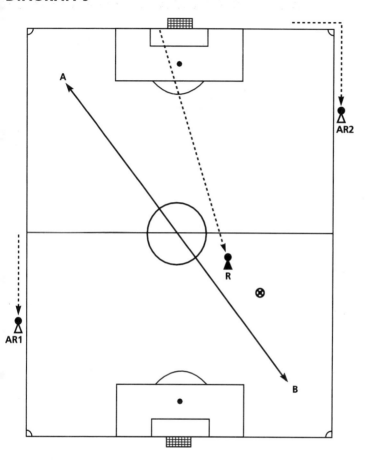

THE COUNTER-ATTACK

(Following Diagram 4)

Referee (R) sprints to regain correct position on diagonal along
path ———→
(Note: The Referee who is physically fit is able to do this easily.)
Assistant Referee (AR2) hurries back to his correct position on the touch-
line.
Assistant Referee (AR1) level with attack and in position to see infringements
and indicate decisions until Referee regains his position.

DIAGRAM 6

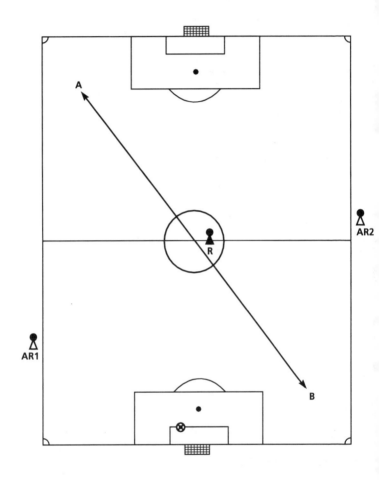

GOAL KICK

Referee (R) in midfield adjacent to central point of diagonal.
Assistant Referee (AR1) exercising watch over goal kick.
Assistant Referee (AR2) in position pending a possible attack by side taking goal kick.

DIAGRAM 7

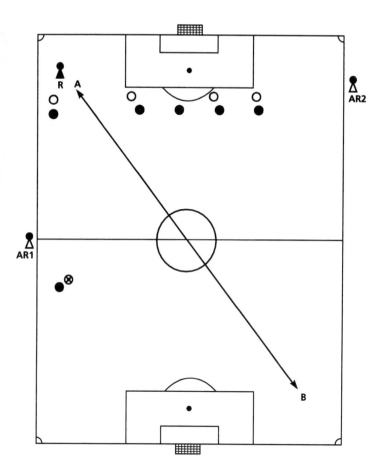

FREE KICK IN MIDFIELD

Players lined up for kick ● and ○. Referee (R) and Assistant Referee (AR2)
in respective diagonal positions, level with players and able to judge
accurately any questions of offside or foul play. Assistant Referee (AR1)
sees that kick is taken from correct position and also is in position for
possible counter attack.

DIAGRAM 8

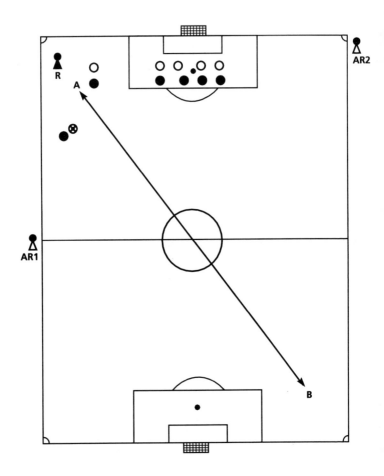

FREE KICK NEAR GOAL

(Just outside penalty-area)

Players ● and ○ line up for free kick.

Referee (R) takes up his position just off his diagonal so that he is placed accurately to judge offside. Assistant Referee (AR2) is more advanced but can watch for offside and fouls and also is in a good position to act as goal judge in the event of a direct shot being taken.

DIAGRAM 9

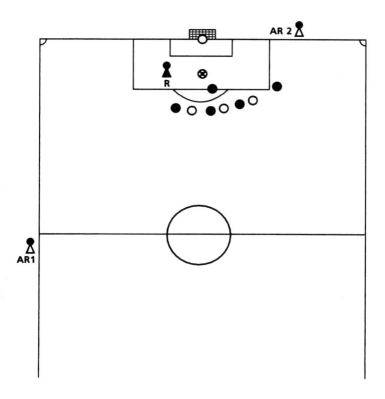

AR 2

R

AR1

PENALTY KICK

Players ● and ○ with the exception of the goalkeeper and kicker are shown outside the penalty area and at least 9.15 m from the ball – goalkeeper on goal line.

Referee (R) is in position to see that kick is properly taken and that no encroachment takes place.

Assistant Referee (AR2) watches goalkeeper to see that he does not advance illegally and also acts as goal judge.

Assistant Referee (AR1) is in position should the goalkeeper save a goal and start a counter attack.

DIAGRAM 10 (A)

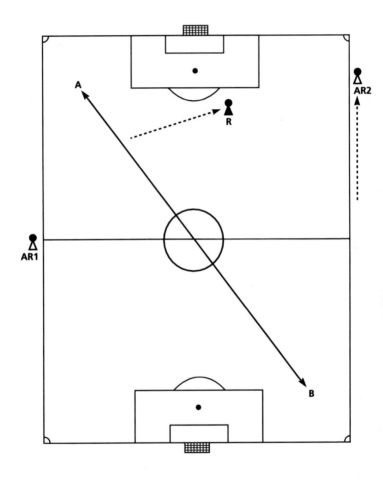

THROW-IN

Ball out of play and Assistant Referee (AR2) is in position to indicate position of throw and to which side.

Referee (R) crosses from diagonal to centre of field, in the same manner as a defence covering a throw-in.

Assistant Referee (AR1) watches his forward line against the possible counter attack.

DIAGRAM 10 (B)

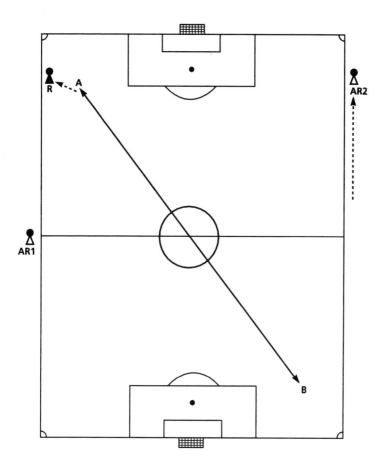

THROW-IN

Assistant Referee (AR1) is away from the throw-in but should be able to judge feet and probably to indicate which side is entitled to throw. He also maintains his position in the event of a clearance.

Referee (R) can judge other throw-in infringements and veers slightly from his diagonal towards touch line.

Assistant Referee (AR2) is in position to see any infringement occurring before Referee can turn to follow play.

NOTE: The players marked ⊗ are attacking the goal and those marked ○ are defending.

Direction of movement of the ball ――――→

Direction of movement of player ―――→

DIAGRAM 1 – OFFSIDE

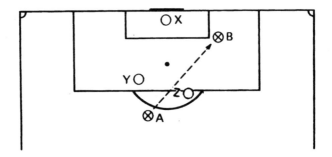

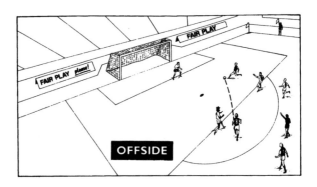

Pass to a Team Mate

The attacker **B** who receives the ball from his team-mate **A** is offside since he is nearer to his opponents' goal line than the ball and the second last defender and gains an advantage by being in that position.

DIAGRAM 2 – NOT OFFSIDE

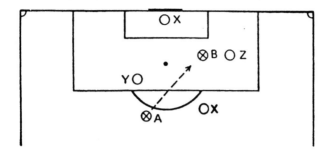

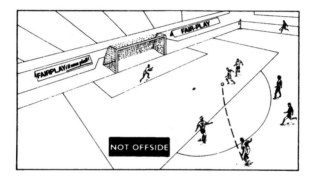

Pass to a Team Mate (continued)

The attacker **B** who receives the ball from his team-mate **A** is not offside because, when the ball is kicked, he is level with the second last defender.

DIAGRAM 3 – NOT OFFSIDE

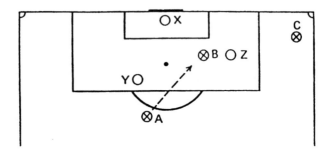

Pass to a Team Mate

The attacker **B** is not offside because, when the ball is played to him by his team-mate **A**, he is level with the second last defender.

The player **C** lying outside the penalty area is in an offside position but would not be penalised since he is not involved in active play.

DIAGRAM 4 – OFFSIDE

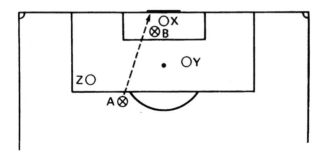

Interfering with an Opponent

The attacker **B** standing in front of the goalkeeper is offside because he is involved in active play and is interfering with an opponent.

DIAGRAM 5 – NOT OFFSIDE

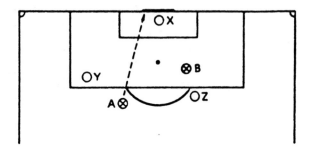

Shot at Goal

Although the attacker **B** is in an offside position when the ball is kicked by his team-mate **A**, he is not penalised because he is not involved in active play and does not gain an advantage by being in that position.

DIAGRAM 6 – OFFSIDE

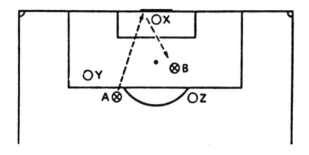

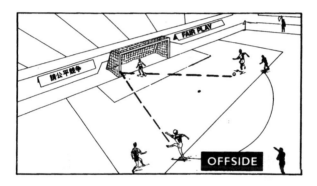

Ball Rebounding from Goal Posts or Crossbar

A shot from **A** rebounds from the goal post to a team-mate **B** who is penalised for being in an offside position because, when the ball is played, he is involved in active play and gains an advantage by being in that position.

DIAGRAM 7 – NOT OFFSIDE

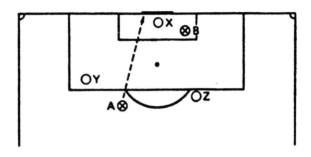

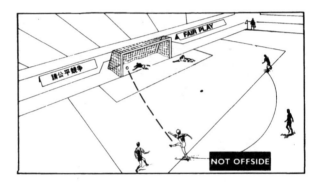

Not Interfering with an Opponent

The player **B** lying in the goal area is not offside since he is not involved in active play and is not interfering with the goalkeeper.

DIAGRAM 8 – OFFSIDE

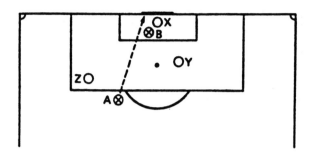

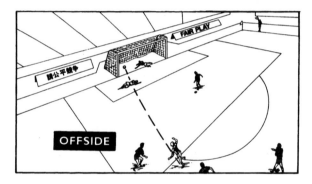

Interfering with an Opponent

The player **B** lying in the goal area is offside because he is in an offside position and is interfering with the goalkeeper.

DIAGRAM 9 – OFFSIDE

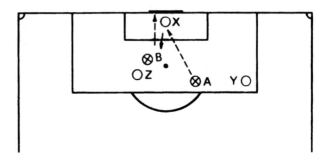

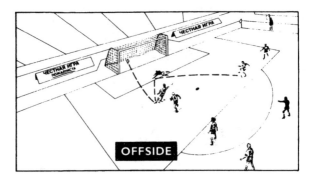

Shot Rebounds from Goalkeeper

A shot from **A** rebounds from the goalkeeper and the team-mate **B** of the attacker is penalised for being in an offside position because, when the ball is played, he is involved in active play and gains an advantage by being in that position.

DIAGRAM 10 – NOT OFFSIDE

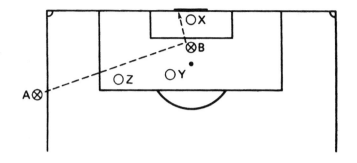

Throw-in

A player cannot be offside from a throw-in.

DIAGRAM 11(a), (b) – NOT OFFSIDE

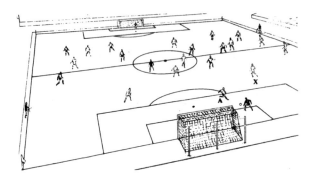

(a) The ball is kicked to the goalkeeper by a team-mate **X** and an attacking player **A** moves to challenge him.

(b) The goalkeeper kicks the ball upfield and the attacking player **A** turns to take up an onside position.

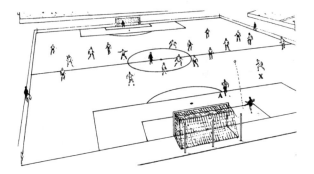

DIAGRAM 11(c) – NOT OFFSIDE

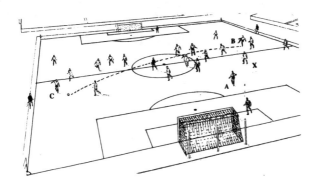

(c) The ball is intercepted by player **B**, a team-mate of the attacking player and played to another team-mate, player **C**, on the wing.

The attacking player **A** is not penalised for being in an offside position because he is not involved in active play and does not gain an advantage from being in that position.

Diagrams illustrating some aspects of denying obvious goalscoring opportunities

I

An attacker is moving towards goal with an obvious goal-scoring opportunity when he is tripped by a defender.

The defender is sent off for denying an opponent a goal-scoring opportunity.

2

An attacker is making his way towards goal when he is tripped by a defender.

He does not have an obvious goal-scoring opportunity, however, and the defender is not sent off.

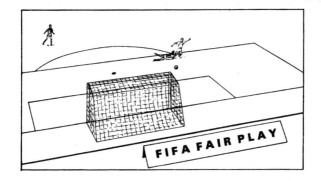

An attacker is making his way to goal when he is held by the goalkeeper.

The goalkeeper is sent off for denying an opponent an obvious goal-scoring opportunity.

The goalkeeper pulls down an attacking player inside his penalty area and a penalty kick is awarded.

The goalkeeper is not sent off since the attacking player is moving away from goal and does not have an obvious goal-scoring opportunity.

An attacker is tripped by a defender inside the penalty area and a penalty kick is awarded.

The defender is not sent off because the attacker is moving away from goal and does not have an obvious goal-scoring opportunity.

An attacking player is moving forward near the touch line when he is tripped by a defender.

The attacking player does not have an obvious goal-scoring opportunity and so the defender is not sent off.

7

An attacker shoots the ball towards goal. Just before it crosses the goal line into goal a defender punches the ball over the bar.

A penalty kick is awarded and the defender is sent off for denying the opposing team a goal.

8

A defender intentionally handles the ball inside his own penalty area and the referee awards a penalty kick.

He does not send off the defender since no obvious goal-scoring opportunity has been denied. If the ball strikes the defender accidentally, no offence has been committed.

9

The ball is played towards goal by the attacking team and a defender jumps and handles it as the attacking player moves towards the ball.

The defender is sent off for denying the opposing team an obvious goal-scoring opportunity.

10

The ball is played forward to an attacking player and the goalkeeper handles it outside the penalty area.

The goalkeeper is sent off for denying the opposing team an obvious goal-scoring opportunity.

Code	Title	Price
	SOCCER TACTICS & SKILLS VIDEOS	
VID001	Attacking in the Attacking 3rd of the Field	£23.44
VID002	Passing & Support	£23.44
VID003	Creating Space	£23.44
VID004	Defending	£23.44
VID005	Defending & Attacking Free Kicks & Corners	£23.44
VID006	Shooting	£23.44
VID007	Goalkeeping	£23.44
VID008	Complete Set – Including a free copy of book	£164.08
	THE WINNING FORMULA VIDEOS	
VID010	Direct Play	£11.99
VID011	Scoring	£11.99
VID012	Winning the Advantage	£11.99
VID013	Defending to Win	£11.99
VID014	Goalkeeping	£11.99
VID015	Complete Set	£49.95
REF001	The Role of the Referee/Fitness Training	£34.66
REF002	Use of the Penalty Mark/Judging Challenges	£34.66
VID020	Soccer Star Video	£10.95

All these video tapes and all publications are available from:–
FA Publications,
9 Wyllyotts Place,
Potters Bar,
Herts. EN6 2JD.

Payment may be made by credit card (Visa/Access/Amex/ Switch)
by telephoning 'FA Publications' on 01707 651840 or faxing on 01707 644190.

Publications 1998/99

Code	Title	Price
	PUBLICATIONS	
PUB006	Soccer Tactics & Skills	£12.99
PUB007	The Winning Formula	£9.99
PUB019	Coaching & Teaching with Disabilities	£2.95
PUB010	Soccer Star Book	£3.00
PUB018	Soccer Star Challenge Pack	£3.00
NVQ001	Football Curriculum Guide	£9.50
PUB001	FA Diary 1998/99 (Available August '98)	£3.99
PUB002	FA Yearbook 1998/99	£7.99
PUB003	FA Handbook 1998/99	£5.00
PUB011	Laws of Association Football (Ref. Chart)	£5.50
PUB012	Arrangement of Fixtures	£1.00
PUB013	Know The Game Soccer	£3.99
PUB015	Flying Start Soccer (hard cover)	£6.50
PUB016	Flying Start Soccer (soft cover)	£2.95
PUB024	Soccer Referee's Manual	£10.99